W9-BMU-740

I Want to Know™

About the CHURCH

Rick Osborne and K.Christie Bowler

ZondervanPublishingHouse

Grand Rapids, Michigan

A Division of HarperCollins Publishers

10

For Lightwave
Managing Editor: Elaine Osborne
Art Director: Terry Van Roon

Photos on pages 14, 18, 21 and 23 courtesy of Zondervan Publishing House.
The photos used on pages 2, 3, 6, 8, 10, 17, 18, 27 and 28 were obtained from Corel Corporation's Professional Photo CD collection.
The images used on pages 5 and 9 were obtained from Adobe Systems Incorporated.
The images used on page 4 and 29 were obtained from ISMI's Master Photos Collection, 1895 Francisco Blvd. East, San Rafael, CA 94901-5506, USA.

Library of Congress Cataloging-in-Publication Data

Osborne, Rick, 1961– .
    The church : what the church is, what it does, and why it's important to me / Rick Osborne and K. Christie Bowler.
        p.   cm.—(I want to know™)
    Summary: Introduces basic concepts about Christianity and the church. Includes suggestions for games and other activities to reinforce understanding.
    ISBN 0–310–22094–7 (hardcover)
    1. Church—Juvenile literature. 2. Christianity—Juvenile literature.   [1. Church. 2. Christianity.] I. Bowler, K. Christie 1958– . II. Title. III. Series: Osborne, Rick, 1961– . I want to know™.
    BV602.5.O73   1998
    262—dc21   98-17209
                                                      CIP
                                                      AC

This edition is printed on acid-free paper and meets the American National Standards Institute Z39.48 standard.

Published by Zondervan Publishing House, Grand Rapids, Michigan 49530, U.S.A. http://www.zondervan.com

Printed in Mexico.

LIGHTWAVE
Building Christian faith in families

A Lightwave Production
P.O. Box 160 Maple Ridge
B.C., Canada V2X 7G1
98 99 00 /DR/ 5 4 3 2 1

Contents

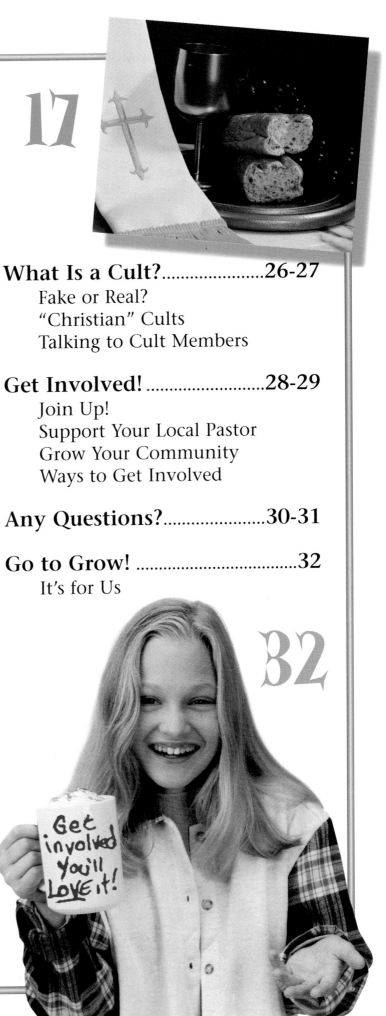

What Is Church?

Join the Club

Did you know you can be part of a "club" that includes people who lived almost 2000 years ago and people who haven't even been born yet? It's called the *church* and includes everyone who has ever believed or will believe in Jesus Christ. (These believers are called *Christians*.) Talk about a big club!

To find out more, we need to go to the book that tells us about the church, what it is, and how it should work. The Bible is the book God gave us so we could learn about him and his plans. It also tells the story of the people who started the first churches.

The Local Club

The Bible tells us that the church is made up of people. It has two parts: the whole church, made up of all Christians; and local groups of believers who meet together. Think about it like this: The world is full of billions of human beings. But we don't all live together. Some of us live in Toronto, some in New York. Others live in Paris or London. In the same way, it's impossible to get together with Christians who have died or haven't been born yet.

And it's impossible to get together with all the Christians alive right now. So we meet in smaller groups. We each belong to a local part of the enormous club made up of all Christians.

You probably think of church as the building you go to on Sunday. Not! The Bible never uses the word for church to mean a building! *Church* always means "groups of believers." *People* are the church. But we have to meet somewhere. Since we're the church wherever we are, people started calling the places we meet churches, too. No problem! Just remember that the church is the people!

All for One

The Bible gives us pictures to help us understand what the church is like. These pictures show that each Christian is an important part of the church. That means you. Yes, *you!* If you are a believer, "You also are like living stones. As you come to [Jesus] you are being built into a house for worship" (1 Peter 2:5). "The whole building is held together by him. It rises to become a holy temple because it belongs to the Lord. And because you belong to him, you too are being built together. You are being made into a house where God lives through his Spirit" (Ephesians 2:21–22).

What happens when you take a brick or two out of a wall? It gets weaker and might even fall down. Each brick is important. And each believer (that's you) is needed to make the whole church strong!

The Bible also says the church is like a body (1 Corinthians 12:12–27) and each of us is a part. We know that every part of our bodies is important. Try to imagine life without a stomach, toes, or elbows! All of us, like all body parts, are needed for the church body to work properly.

Every brick in the building, every part of the body, every believer in the church is important.

Like pieces of a mosaic, together Christians form the body of Christ.

Church Is God's Idea

It's Your Family

Okay, we're part of the church. Cool. But what does that mean? Whose idea was it? And why should we go? That's kind of like asking who thought up families and wondering why we should be part of one. Your family is made up of you, your parents, and your brothers and sisters. You're born into a family—that's just part of being human. And it's just the beginning.

God designed families so that, as we grow and learn, we can have great relationships with our brothers, sisters, and parents. It's not always easy, but it's worth it! We get to know them, and they get to know us. No matter what we do, they love us. Through disagreements, good times, and rough spots, we love them. These are life-long

relationships! Families also support each other through all life's stuff. We're there for each other. We go to each other's concerts and games. We're proud of each other when we do well and encourage each other when we don't.

That's what God's idea for the church is. When we become Christians, we're born into the church family. Our church family loves and supports us as we grow as Christians and go through all the things life brings. Church, like family, should be a wonderful, encouraging, friendly place to be.

It's for Love

God is love, so everything he does comes from love. When he gave us the church, he did it out of love for us. He planned it all so that we would be loved, cared for, supported, trained, and encouraged. In fact, church is all about God's two greatest commandments: Love God with all of who you are; love each other as you love yourselves.

We can never out-love God. Loving him is the best thing we can do! When we love God, we get to know him and grow a relationship with him. That relationship becomes the greatest blessing in our lives because he's the greatest Friend. And as we love each other, we get to know others, and they get to know us. Those relationships become great blessings, too. So we have a God who loves us, knows us inside out, and takes care of us. And we have friends who love us, enjoy being with us, and cheer us on—just as we do for them.

Church is God's gift!

It's in the Bible

God made it pretty clear that church was his idea—just read the New Testament! (That's the part of the Bible about Jesus and his disciples, who became the first believers.) The church is a huge topic! Check this out:

- Jesus talked about his church before it even started (Matthew 16:18)!
- *Acts* tells us about the Holy Spirit starting and organizing churches.
- The apostle Paul, an important leader, spent most of his time starting and helping churches.
- Most of the New Testament is letters to churches. They say how the church should work, tell how everyone has a part to play, and teach about church membership, discipline, and unity.
- *James* (Jesus' brother) tells us to call for church leaders if we're sick. He even talks about seating arrangements (James 5:14–15; 2:1–9)!
- *Hebrews* commands us to obey church leaders and keep meeting with other Christians (Hebrews 13:17; 10:25).

The Story of the Church

The Beginning

The church started when people began believing in Jesus and needed leaders and other believers to help them grow. Jesus knew God's plan for the church, so he trained the first leaders—his disciples. Jesus told them about the plan: He would die, taking the penalty for everyone's sins, then the Holy Spirit would come, make them God's children, and live with and in them (John 14:17).

After he was killed, Jesus rose from the dead on a Sunday. He appeared to his followers on a Sunday. Seven weeks after Jesus rose, God sent the Holy Spirit and the church began—on a Sunday. (That's why we meet on Sunday.) That Sunday, Jews from all over the Roman Empire were in Jerusalem for the Feast of Pentecost. All Jesus' followers were together. With a sound like a big wind the Holy Spirit came. Flames appeared over the disciples' heads, and the Spirit filled each of them! People ran to see what had happened. When Peter told them about Jesus, over 3000 believed, and the church began!

Paul went to synagogues to tell the Jews about Jesus. Jews still meet in synagogues today.

First Steps

After the feast, many new believers left Jerusalem for home, taking the story of Jesus with them. Meanwhile, in Jerusalem, the disciples talked about Jesus and did miracles like healing the sick. People saw their actions and listened to them. The religious leaders didn't want them to talk about Jesus and ordered them to stop. But the disciples refused.

The religious leaders said the believers were lying about God. People turned against the believers. Soon they were being imprisoned or even killed! Many ran away from Jerusalem carrying the message with them. Soon groups of believers were starting local churches in towns all around Jerusalem. The church was growing!

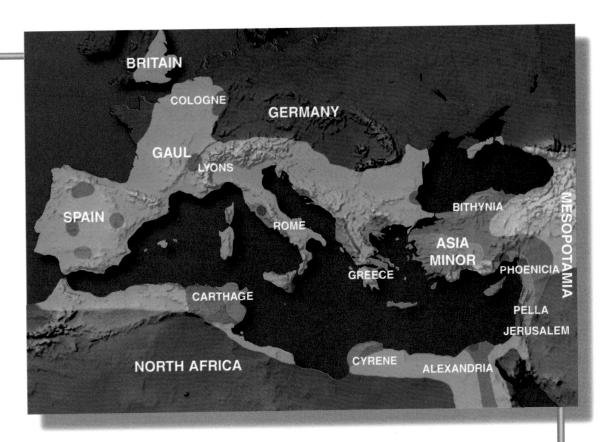

The spread of the church from A.D. 0–A.D. 325.

LEGEND

- by A.D. 45
- by A.D. 100
- by A.D. 185
- by A.D. 325

Growth Spurt!

One religious leader, Saul, arrested any believers he could find. He even traveled to Damascus searching for more. On the way, Jesus appeared and told him the truth—Jesus was God's Son. Saul (also called Paul) believed and went to Antioch to help train the believers. (They were first called Christians there.) Later the Antioch church sent him to tell people all over the Roman Empire about God's plan.

Whenever Paul arrived in a town, he went to the Jewish meeting place. Sometimes, when he told the Jews about Jesus, they believed. Other times they threw him out. Then Paul would talk to non-Jews. They didn't have good meeting places so they gathered in homes to listen. Paul started local churches like these everywhere he went.

Soon the church had grown from a few disciples meeting in one place to thousands of believers meeting all across the Roman Empire. Talk about a growth spurt!

First Church Buildings

Christians met in homes for some time because it was too dangerous to build public meeting places. The Jewish religious leaders were against them. And, because they wouldn't worship the Roman Emperor, the Romans were against them. It wasn't until Christianity became legal, around A.D. 323, that Christians could build their own public meeting places.

The oldest church building we know about, and can still see part of, was combined with a home! In A.D. 231, in a town called Dura-Europos (now Salhiyeh, Iraq), a Christian added a room onto his home that could hold about a hundred people. He also added a brick bath to baptize people in.

Church and Worship

ing ourselves to God in response to who he is! Jesus said, "God is spirit. His worshipers must worship him in spirit and in truth" (John 4:24). That means worshiping him honestly from our hearts, with our whole lives and all of who we are. We can worship God anytime on our own, but getting together with other Christians encourages us to give more of ourselves to God.

The Circle of Worship

Start with God: Everything God does comes from love. When we come together and learn about God, we realize we can trust him: He keeps his promises, knows everything, can do anything, is everywhere, and always loves us. So—we're never alone, there's no problem too big for God, and he understands everything we face.

God also *acts* loving! We remind each other of what he's done—in the Bible and for us. He helped us once, he'll do it again. "God did not spare his own Son. He gave him up for us all. Then won't he also freely give us everything else?" (Romans 8:32).

Praise/Thanks: The more we know God and see him working in our lives, the more grateful we are. We praise him individually and together. Praise is simply thanking God for how great he is.

Risky Worship!

On a starry night, Christians secretly enter a simple house. If they're caught, they could be imprisoned or killed—just for being Christians! Throughout history, and today in countries where Christian meetings are illegal, Christians take the risk.

Why? What's so important about church? For one thing, *worship*—giv-

Commitment: As we praise God together, we realize how wonderful he is and we give him more control of our lives, asking for help to trust, love, and serve him more. We worship him by wanting to get closer and commit our lives to him. That brings us full circle.

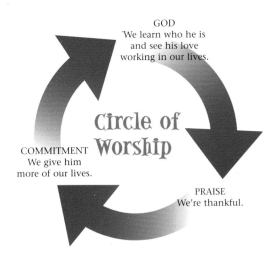

GOD
We learn who he is and see his love working in our lives.

Circle of Worship

COMMITMENT
We give him more of our lives.

PRAISE
We're thankful.

Back to God: God responds to our worship by changing us, growing us more like Jesus, and doing even more in our lives. As we learn more about him, our *praise* comes from deeper inside us. When we get together and tell each other how wonderful he is and what he's doing we're led to even deeper *commitment* to God as we want him in our lives more. We're encouraged to worship God more and have him bring us closer to him.

Each time around this worship circle we go a little deeper into relationship with God. We become more like Jesus, we're more sure that God loves us, and we're encouraged by what he's doing. Our whole lives change. Worship becomes natural and wonderful as we see and know his love more.

And that's worth getting together for—even when it's risky.

Ways We Worship

No two families do things the same. Each uses ways that work for them. It's the same with churches. Groups of Christians express their worship differently. Some use upbeat music, others use hymns. Some sing loudly, some softly. Some have choirs, some have bands. Some raise their hands. Some kneel. Some clap. But we all give our lives, wills, hearts, and minds to God—as individuals and as groups. No matter how we express our worship, we're all part of God's church!

Church Is for Friends and Community

Community Center

Church is also about people! Walk around your neighborhood. You'll probably see a school, maybe a community hall or recreation building, perhaps a church. You'll see faces you know. This is your *community*—the place you're involved and know people. Parts of your community might be outside your neighborhood. It's easy to get involved in places far away because most people have cars. Perhaps you drive to church. In the early days, church was always nearby because the only travel was by foot or donkey. How long would it take you to walk to church at three miles an hour?

Back then, church was full of neighbors. That worked well, because church provides us with community—a safe place where people know us, watch us grow, give us advice, and help us. Church is full of people who care about us and who we care about. Our church is our community center where we take care of each other. It's our Christian family!

When we come together and do what God says—help and love each other, care for the sick and poor—what Jesus said comes true. "If you love one another, everyone will know you are my disciples" (John 13:35). People notice and want to join!

Friends Like Us

Church is a good place to find friends. If you want to play baseball do you hang out with hockey players? Not likely! We enjoy being around people interested in the same things we are. That way we can help each other learn, practice, and improve. Being a Christian is the same. If we want to follow God, we'll hang out with people who go to church. If we want to understand the Bible, we'll hang around with people interested in the Bible. We become like those we spend our time with. Choose good friends carefully (Proverbs 22:24–25)!

The best place to find friends is in our Christian community: our church, Christian school, or Christian clubs. Look for people who (1) share your values and like what you like, (2) want to know God as much as you do, and (3) can help you make good decisions. When your best friends are believers, you will grow together into strong, happy Christians.

There's nothing wrong with having non-Christian friends, but they shouldn't be our closest friends. Tell them how wonderful God is and how great being a Christian is. Maybe they'll become one—especially if they see a difference in your life!

Good Friends

Ask God to help you be a *Proverbs* friend—and have great friendships!

Be loyal—"Don't desert your friends or your parents' friends" (Proverbs 27:10).

Be honest—"Those who are honest have respect for the Lord" (14:2). "Don't let love and truth ever leave you" (3:3).

Give good advice—"Perfume and incense bring joy to your heart. And friends are sweeter when they give you honest advice" (27:9).

Get along—"Avoiding a fight brings you honor" (20:3). "Wise people keep themselves under control" (29:11).

Forgive—"Those who erase a sin by forgiving it show love" (17:9).

Love—"Friends love at all times" (17:17). "Everybody longs for love that never fails" (19:22).

Be kind—"Pleasant words are like honey. They are sweet to the spirit and bring healing to the body" (16:24).

The Church Is for Teaching and Reaching Out

Training Coaches

Imagine being in a club where you don't know the rules. Or playing a sport without knowing how and with no coach to help. Pretty tough, huh? That's like trying to live as a Christian without knowing God's principles or what the truth is.

God knew we'd need help so he gave us church leaders and coaches—pastors, Sunday school teachers, and others who have spent years getting to know God and studying the Bible. The Bible has everything we need to know about living God's way! It trains us to do right, teaches us what's true, and helps us see our mistakes (2 Timothy 3:16–17).

Church leaders coach us. They train us for the life God wants, teach us the Bible, and help us understand what we believe and what God expects. They explain the truth and teach us how to study the Bible for ourselves. Soon we'll be explaining it to others!

Learning to be a Christian isn't like cramming for a test. It's more like learning skills for a sport. We have to know how to *use* what we learn. Our coaches help us apply it. The goal is to grow, change, and become more like Jesus. He was kind, loving, and selfless, and always obeyed God. Awesome!

As coaches train their players to be the best, God has given us lots of people to coach us to live the best Christian lives we can.

Spreading the Love

This growing more like Jesus isn't just for us. No way! When we're filled with God's love, we want to spread it around. God gave leaders to his church "so that they might prepare God's people to serve" (Ephesians 4:12). God wants us to become mature and learn to serve and help others. God's love fills our hearts so full it spills over. We then reach out, individually and as a community, and love people. Suddenly they want to know Jesus, too!

Churches often use soup kitchens, food banks, giving to the poor, visiting the sick, and events like Christmas banquets to reach the neighborhood. Get involved! We can love, help, and be kind to our friends, people we meet, or other students. When they see our loving actions, they'll want to know what makes us different. Then we can explain about God's love, telling them how wonderful he is and how much he loves us all. We can tell them about Jesus and invite them to join the club.

Churches often help people in other parts of the world, too. Maybe your church sponsors a missionary, sends supplies to needy people, or supports an orphanage. Find out what your church is doing and take part. Spread God's love around!

Just as Paul taught Timothy and Titus, so do church leaders coach us and help us understand the Bible.

Wise Advice

Other Christians in our church community are a great safety net! When we figure out a solution to a problem, or think we've got everything straight, we should bounce our idea off other Christians. They'll help keep us on track. God has given us these people for a reason. Often they see things we don't. Or they've tried something and know it won't work.

If these wise Christians tell you not to do something, ask why, and be willing to take their advice. It could save you trouble! "Wise children pay attention to what their parents [and other wise leaders] tell them" (Proverbs 13:1). "Plans fail without good advice. But they succeed when there are many advisers" (Proverbs 15:22).

Understanding Your Church Service

The Basics

Think "restaurant." Which one? There are all kinds. They have different names, designs, menus, and specials. But they all share the basics that make them restaurants—they serve yummy food and delicious drinks!

The whole church is made up of a variety of local churches. Each one is different in some way, with its own look, sound, and style. But all churches are the same in the important ways, like sharing the basic things that make them Christian. For example, they all believe and follow God's word in the Bible. They all encourage people to "practice" Christian living and grow more like Jesus. They all worship the same God.

Also, churches have the same basic elements in their services.

How many things can you find that Christians do in church?

Singing/"Worship": Our services often start with singing. (Check out *Psalms* in the Bible for some of King David's songs.) We've been worshiping God all week as we respond to his love. As we come together, music helps focus our hearts and minds on God's goodness and character. It leads us as individuals and as a group into praise, thanks, and greater commitment to God. The words of the songs express our hearts to God and prepare us for the rest of the service.

Prayer: Talking to God together reminds us of God's care and love. We bring our church community's needs to God and support each other in prayer. We praise God and confess our sins. Prayer also reminds us that God is with us, listening!

Offering/Tithe: The whole world is God's! He gives us everything we have. In thanks, we give some back to him. Some call this giving back an offering and some call it a tithe. Tithe can mean "a **T**enth **I**n **T**hanks to **H**im for **E**verything!" The church uses this money to pay the bills and the pastors, to support missions and care for the needy. Since church is our community center, our "home away from home," we are responsible to care for it—with our money and ourselves!

Teaching/Preaching: The sermon helps us understand what being a Christian is all about. It helps us know God more and understand the

The bread and wine of Communion remind us that Jesus died for us.

Bible. It encourages us to read and study our Bible on our own. We should always go to church expecting God to teach us. When we do, it's amazing what we learn and how we grow!

Baptism: Jesus commanded his disciples to baptize people. Baptism reminds us that Jesus washed away our sins. It's a sign that we commit our lives to God and have been accepted into his church.

Communion/Lord's Supper: The foundation of our lives as Christians is Jesus Christ and what he did for us. "Communion," the "Lord's Supper," or the "Eucharist," reminds us of that. Jesus said, "This is my body. It is given for you. Every time you eat it, do it in memory of me. This cup is the new covenant in my blood. It is poured out for you" (Luke 22:19–20). By taking part in this wonderful ceremony we're remembering that Jesus died for us.

Why So Many Churches?

Mammals and Churches?

What do elephants and rabbits, horses and bears, puppy dogs and marmosets have in common? They share characteristics that make them mammals instead of reptiles or birds: They have hair, give birth to live babies, and breast-feed their young. But they're also different—shapes and sizes, fur and toeses, ears and noses.

In a similar way, churches share key things that make them Christian, but there are many ways they're different. The main characteristic of Christian churches is that they agree on basic doctrines or truths. (For example, they believe Jesus was God's Son who died for us and rose again.) Every Christian believes the *Apostles' Creed.* "Creed" means "I believe." The Apostles' Creed is a summary of the apostles' teaching that's been around for 1700 years!

Horse or Elephant?

There are almost as many kinds of Christian churches as there are mammals! If we all believe the same things, why are churches so different? God loves variety! His different people act and express themselves differently. Here are three main ways:

Churches express their love for God differently.

What they emphasize: A lot of people agree dogs are great. But some like dobermans, others prefer terriers or mutts. Churches are like that, too. They agree on the main truths but have favorite ones. Some churches love talking about Jesus and helping people meet him. Their services give people a chance to make that decision. Other churches emphasize the Bible and often focus on studying and applying it. Others emphasize the Holy Spirit, growing as Christians, or helping the poor.

How they express themselves: You think and act as you do partly because you were brought up in a North American culture and democracy. Churches started and grew in different cultures and styles of government. Some have hundreds of years of tradition and history behind them. Their services are similar to how they've always been. Other churches came out of traditions from various cultures around the world. Others are still figuring out their own traditions. All this affects how they express themselves. For example, music (hymns or choruses? organs or electric guitars?); leaders' dress (robes, suits, or jeans?); people's parts in the service (clap hands or sit quietly? written-out words or chosen in the moment?).

How they view other doctrines: Churches also observe *secondary* or less important doctrines differently:

Communion—is it served at the front by the priest or in your seat by ushers? Healing—do they talk about it a lot and regularly pray for the sick or hardly at all?

All these things make churches seem very different. But remember, we all belong to God! He loves every one of us. When we get to know people from other churches, we should focus on our similarities, not our differences. We should love and care for each other, no matter what Christian church we go to. The beauty of having so many churches is that everyone can find one they love and fit into perfectly!

The Apostles' Creed

We believe in God the Father Almighty,
    maker of heaven and earth;
And in Jesus Christ his only Son,
    our Lord;
    who was conceived by the Holy Spirit,
    born of the Virgin Mary,
        suffered under Pontius Pilate,
    was crucified, dead, and buried;
    he descended into hell;
    the third day he rose again
        from the dead;
    he ascended into heaven,
    and sits on the right hand of God,
        the Father Almighty;
    from there he shall come to
        judge the living and the dead.
We believe in the Holy Spirit,
    the holy Christian church,
    the communion of saints,
    the forgiveness of sins,
    the resurrection of the body,
    and the life everlasting.
        Amen.

Church History

There Was One, Then There Were Two

Ever been on a team where the members agree on everything? Not likely! It's easy to forget we're working for the same goal. All Christians belong to God's church and believe the Apostles' Creed, but sometimes we forget that. Church history is full of disagreements.

At the beginning there was only one *Catholic Church* ("catholic" means universal). At that time the Roman Empire was against Christians. It persecuted and killed them until A.D. 323, when *Constantine* became emperor. He made Christianity legal. Over the next several hundred years the church grew like crazy. The leaders met several times to discuss the Bible's doctrines. During this time the Apostles' Creed was written, and great Christian leaders like *Augustine* wrote books explaining the important Christian doctrines to ordinary people.

Sadly, over the years, greedy men found they could get rich leading churches. More interested in money and power than God, they bought positions as church leaders!

Meanwhile, the churches in Rome and Constantinople disagreed about certain beliefs and about who should rule all the churches. Finally,

Unscramble the letters of the names to find out who these men of church history were.

HONJ LAVNIC

STANCOTINEN

NIGK YEHNR IVII

OPPE OLE X

NOHJ SLEWEY

in 1054, the two groups split into the *Roman Catholic Church* led by Rome and the *Eastern Orthodox Church* led by Constantinople.

Reform the Church!

The Catholic Church started selling certificates called *indulgences* that let you get out of doing *penance* (what priests told you to do to make up for sinning). Greedy church leaders became very rich selling indulgences.

Along came *Martin Luther!* He believed the church needed to be *reformed* or returned to how it used to be—following God, not money. He said indulgences and penance made people not care about sin because they thought they could buy forgiveness and save themselves without needing Jesus. In 1517, Luther wrote ninety-five arguments against indulgences. Later, he wrote about Romans 5:1, "We have been made right with God because of our faith." That means we're saved from our sins because of what Jesus did, not because of anything we do. Luther also believed the Bible was above the Pope. This made the Pope angry. In 1521 *Pope Leo X* excommunicated or kicked Luther out of the Roman Catholic Church.

Luther's teachings caught on anyway. His followers, *Lutherans,* and others, split from the Catholic Church. They came to be called *Protestants* because they "protested"

that the Bible, not the Pope, was the most important authority on God and the Christian life. The *Reformation* of the church had begun!

Martin Luther

More books have been written about Luther (who lived from 1483–1546) than any other person except Jesus! Luther studied law, then, after almost being killed by lightning, he became a priest. He wasn't sure he was saved from his sins until he realized he was forgiven through faith in what Jesus had done. What a relief! This changed his life—and the church—forever!

The people loved Luther's message! He translated the Bible into German so they could read it, and he kept writing and preaching. Luther taught: (1) Jesus alone saves us from our sins; (2) The Bible alone teaches the truth; (3) Faith alone, not what we do, saves us.

Luther received death threats. To save his life, a friend kidnaped him and disguised him as a knight! Luther caused the Reformation in Europe. What if there'd been no lightning and he'd become a lawyer instead of a priest?

More Church History

More Protesters

Leaving the Catholic Church was contagious! As people left, the Catholic Church began reforming itself. *Pope Paul III* made laws that helped stop the greed. And groups like the *Jesuits,* who focused on God and serving others, sprang up.

Everyone started reexamining what Christians are and believe. Forgetting we're all one, people disagreed on secondary doctrines and separated from Luther's followers to start their own churches. Most churches today trace their roots back to this time of reformation.

At that time, churches baptized babies. *Anabaptists* said only people who can decide for themselves to follow God should be baptized. They were re-baptized ("ana" means again). Today's *Mennonites, Baptists, Brethren,* and *Quakers* came out of the Anabaptists.

John Calvin (1509–1564) taught that God chose long ago who would become Christians. His followers, *Calvinists,* started the *Reformed* and *Presbyterian Churches. Jacobus Arminius* (1560–1609) disagreed with Calvin. He said we have a choice whether we follow God or not. His followers, *Arminians,* are often found in other churches like some Baptist groups.

A Method in His Madness

Meanwhile, in England, *King Henry VIII* wanted a divorce. The Pope wouldn't let him so Henry separated the English church from the Catholic Church. It became the *Church of England,* later called the *Anglican Church.* In the United States, the Anglican Church is called the Episcopal Church. In many ways it seems Catholic, but it's led by the Archbishop of Canterbury, not the Pope.

In the early 1700s, *John and Charles Wesley* developed a method for training people in the Christian faith; therefore they were called *Methodists.* John's teaching spread through England and Ireland and came to America in 1760. John's followers were a "society" within the Church of England until they left in 1795.

Newest Movements

In the early 1900s in America, people wanted the Holy Spirit to come as he did in Acts 2 at Pentecost. They emphasized this "baptism of the Holy Spirit" and the gifts the Spirit brought, such as speaking in tongues. Eventually they started their own *Pentecostal* churches. Some people stayed in their old churches but emphasized the Holy Spirit and his gifts (*charisma*). They were called *Charismatics.*

All these churches, and others, have grown and changed over the years. Today they're again focusing more on the Apostles' Creed than the things which divide us. After centuries of disagreements and splits, many churches are putting aside their differences and finding ways to work together. Imagine being separated from your siblings for years because you had a fight. Then you put the fight behind you and you're a family again. That's what's happening to the church! We're remembering we're all God's children.

Augustine

In A.D. 354, not long after Christianity became legal, one of the greatest Christian thinkers was born in North Africa. Augustine wanted to do what was right but couldn't. At first, Christianity didn't make sense to him. Then one day he heard a voice saying, "Pick it up and read." He opened the Bible and read Romans 13:13. It talked about exactly what Augustine was struggling with! He became a Christian and was soon leading the church in Hippo, North Africa. He wrote books explaining Christian doctrines so people would know the truth. We still read those books today!

Interesting Church Buildings

Talk About Old!

Ever since Emperor Constantine, Christians have been building meeting places for themselves. Some church buildings took entire lifetimes to build. Many of these old churches were built so well they're still around hundreds of years later! There's been a church building of some sort where St. Peter's Basilica in Rome is since around A.D. 160! The newest one was built in the 1500s. For centuries, St. Peter's was the biggest church in the world. St. Peter's is part of the *Vatican* where the Pope lives and works. It's called St. Peter's because it's on the place where people think Jesus' disciple Peter was killed and/or buried.

St. Peter's Basilica in Rome, Italy.

Ancient wooden church in Heddal, Norway.

St. Sophia's is a huge church built in Constantinople (now Istanbul in Turkey) by the emperor Justinian. Finished in A.D. 537, the church still stands today. St. Sophia's was so beautiful that when the Turks conquered Constantinople they couldn't destroy it. They turned it into a Moslem mosque instead and still use it!

Talk About Variety!

Churches come in all shapes and sizes. St. Basil's Cathedral in Moscow is a wooden church built in the 1500s. Look at it and you can tell it's different from churches built in western Europe. It's full of color and variety with nine domes and rich decorations. In Scandinavia a different kind of building was popular. Check out the stave church in Heddal, Norway!

A little church in South Woodbury, Vermont.

Churches were built with whatever material was available. In Mexico they were built with adobe, a kind of red mud. In Ethiopia they were carved out of solid rock. And in Hawaii some were built from coral!

Many church buildings were built to be huge and awesome as a way to show God's greatness. These churches were beautifully decorated with pictures, carvings, and stained glass windows.

Taos Pueblo, New Mexico, adobe church.

Did You Know?

The biggest church in the world is the Basilica of Our Lady of Peace in Yamoussoukra, Ivory Coast, West Africa. It was finished in 1989 and has an area of 323,000 square feet* (that's seven football fields)! The smallest church in the world is the chapel of Santa Isabel de Hungria, in Spain. It has an area of 21 ⅛ square feet!† The smallest church in the United States, Union Church at Wiscasset, Maine, is 7 feet long by 4 feet wide.† If you lay across its width, your head and feet might touch both sides!

The oldest church in the United States, built around 1632, is the Newport Parish Church near Smithfield, Virginia.*

The tallest cathedral spire in the world belongs to the Protestant Cathedral in Ulm, Germany. Begun in 1377, the 528-foot high tower wasn't finished until 1890!* If 88 men stood on each other's heads they might reach the top of the tower!

No matter what the church building is like, its main purpose is to provide a place for Christians to come together, worship God, encourage each other, learn more about God, pray for one another, and help those in need. Today, there are still Christians who can't have their own buildings because Christianity is illegal in their countries. So they meet in homes just like the first Christians did!

Where Christianity is illegal, Christians meet in homes.

Saint Basil's Cathedral, Moscow.

*Records from **THE GUINNESS BOOK OF WORLD RECORDS 1998** ©1997 Guinness Publishing Ltd.

†Records from **THE GUINNESS BOOK OF WORLD RECORDS 1990** ©1989 Guinness Publishing Ltd.

What Is a Cult?

Fake or Real?

Say you want to join Boy or Girl Scouts. You find a club called "Boy Scats" and "Girl Goods." Same thing, you think. So you join and discover you have to wear black jeans and purple shirts, eat only asparagus, liver, and popcorn (with extra butter), and drink fruit juice. You must believe the moon is a spaceship and brown eyes are best. Are these Boy or Girl Scouts? Nope! They're fake. You can tell by what they believe and how they act.

There are "fake" churches, too. They're called *cults*.

You can tell the difference between a church and a cult by what they believe and how they tell their members to act. Here's what makes a group a cult.

Wrong Beliefs: A group that disagrees with the basic doctrines in the Apostles' Creed isn't Christian. Sounds straightforward, huh? Cults usually disagree that: God made the universe and cares about us; we're sinners needing forgiveness; the Holy Spirit is God working in the church; or Jesus is God's Son who lived, died for our sins, then rose again. Many cults say Jesus was a good man or great teacher, but not God. But Jesus *is* God! He really did die for us and rise again!

The "Only" Way: Cults teach that they are the only ones who know the truth—God gave it to them. No other group, Christian or otherwise, is right. So you *must* join their group and do or promise certain things.

Obey the Leader: All members of a cult have to obey the leader or founder. Since they alone have the truth, they believe, their leaders speak for God. Cults believe that the leader *never* makes mistakes. And don't question what they teach! Accept it as truth. To cults, the group matters more than the person.

"Christian" Cults

Sometimes a group starts out Christian but gets sidetracked into making a secondary doctrine more important than the Apostles' Creed. Take angels, for example. The Bible tells stories of angels: Angels destroyed Sodom, told Mary she would have God's Son, told Joseph to run away to Egypt, and got Peter out of jail. However, if a church starts teaching that we should worship and follow angels, it has become a cult!

But don't worry! God loves us and wants us to know the truth—he *is* truth! He'll keep us on track. To keep us safe from cults, bad leaders, and wrong teachings, we just need to keep reading the Bible, trusting God, and listening to good Christian leaders.

Talking to Cult Members

What can you do if your friend is in a cult? Lots! (1) Love them and focus on Jesus! Jesus said, "If you love one another, everyone will know you are my disciples" (John 13:35). Most cults care more about rules than love—so they notice our love. (2) God doesn't force anyone. Don't try to force your friend to change. Respect their freedom to choose for themselves. (3) Find out about the cult your friend is in by talking to a knowledgeable adult or reading Christian books about what that cult believes. (4) Pray. Jesus said the truth will set us free. He also said he is the Truth. Pray for God to help your friend know the Truth!

We should follow and worship God, not angels. Angels work for God.

Get Involved!

Join Up!

You've learned a lot about church. So what now? Simple! Get involved. But first you have to join up. Remember the very first step? You need to become a member of God's church by becoming a Christian. That's simple, too. God wants everyone to be welcome. All you need to do is agree that you sin, do wrong things, and need help. Then tell God you believe the Apostles' Creed, you know he made every-thing, and you believe Jesus died for your sins and rose again (John 3:16). Ask God to forgive you, be your Father, and make you his child. That's it! As soon as you believe and pray that, God answers and you're his child (1 John 3:1)! The next step is to find a local church community to help you grow as a Christian.

Support Your Local Pastor

Now that you belong, you need to support your pastors and leaders (1 Thessalonians 5:12–13; Hebrews 13:17). This means giving some of your time, money, and energy. There are always things that need to be done around a church—setting up chairs, helping in the nursery, singing in the choir, teaching Sunday school, or cleaning up. Help your church be a happy, well-run community.

Look for what you're good at. What talents has God given you? What do you love doing? Find ways to do those things whenever you're with other Christians. For example, if you're good at encouraging people, you can do that anywhere, anytime! You don't have to have a formal "job" of encouraging. Just do it! It's the same with other things you're good at. God gives us gifts and talents because his people need them. We all have a part to play (1 Corinthians 12). If we don't do it, it just won't get done!

Grow Your Community

Help build your church community. That means letting people know who you are, getting to know others, and finding new friends at your church. But a community is never all one age. (That would be boring!) So get to know people of all ages, from grandparents to babies. Each one belongs to your community just like you do. They can help you grow, give you wisdom, teach you, and encourage and challenge you. But you can help them, too. Younger children might look to you for advice as a role model. Older people love having younger people around. A community is everyone helping everyone else. What a place!

with your hands? Offer to make something for the Sunday school.

Find out what's going on for your age group and be there! But don't just go—help. You'll get to know people quickly when you're active in the group.

Ways to Get Involved

Let's get specific! Do you have a room at home big enough for your youth group? Ask your parents to let you invite the group over. Are you musical? Join the choir or offer to play your guitar. Do you like cooking? Have a bake sale to raise money for your group! Are you friendly and like meeting new people? Be a greeter who makes people feel welcome. Are you good

Any Questions?

The church has been around for two thousand years—working, growing, changing, and figuring out its job in the world. You've learned a lot in this book, but you've just scratched the surface! Here's a bit more.

Q Why do we go to church if God is everywhere?

A In the Bible, God tells us to join other Christians and worship him. We should spend time alone, praying and reading his Word. But it is also very important to get together with others who follow Christ. We can encourage and strengthen each other. We can pray for each other. We can learn from each other. We can sing and praise God together. We can serve and help each other. All of this can happen in church. Church is also a place where Christians of all ages and types can come together— babies, grandparents, children, poor, wealthy, brown, black, white, American, Asian, African, weak, strong, and so on. Something very special happens when God's family gets together.

Q Why do people get baptized?

A People get baptized because Jesus was baptized, and they want to follow his example. They also get baptized because Jesus told his followers to go into all the world, telling people about him and baptizing them. Some Christians believe that babies from Christian families should be baptized to show that they belong to Christ. Some Christians think that only believers in Christ should be baptized, to show that Jesus is their Savior. Either way, baptism is a very important event in a Christian's life.

BAPTISMAL TANK

Q **What part of the body of Christ am I?**

A The Bible uses word pictures to explain how Christians relate to each other. We are a "family," with brothers and sisters in Christ. We are a "building," with Christ as the cornerstone. We are a "body," with each person serving as a special part. God talks about us being a body to show how Christians should treat each other and work together. God has given each Christian special gifts. That means each of us has talents and abilities that can be used to help other believers. Not everybody has the same gifts. And, like the parts of a body, we need each other. All of our gifts are important.

DRESS REHEARSAL

Q **Why do we worship God?**

A Worship means praising and thanking God for who he is and for what he has done. People worship in many different ways. Worship can involve group singing, group reading, special music, giving money, prayer, Communion, Bible reading, teaching, preaching, and other activities. God has given us everything good that we have. He loves us and wants the very best for us. Shouldn't we spend time with him and tell him how grateful we are? We play with our friends because we enjoy them. We worship God because we enjoy him.

Adapted from *101 Questions Children Ask About God*, The Livingstone Corporation and Lightwave Publishing, 1992.

Go to Grow!

Have you ever put on a surprise party? Do you remember planning for it, then watching it come together? What a feeling when the surprise works and the person is happy! Now try imagining how God feels watching his plans for his church come together. That's your feeling multiplied by zillions! God loves watching us grow together and come to know him more. He loves the way we affect the world around us and how we show others how wonderful he is. That's his plan, after all. The church is important to him. It was his idea from the very beginning.

It's for Us

God loves us. He thought out his idea for church with us in mind. He knew it would help us. He wanted the church to show us who he is and how much he loves and cares for us. Church is a place where we can worship God, and where he can work in our lives, making us happy and meeting our needs. God knew church would be a place where we could find our best friends and learn how to live a great life. So it only makes sense to go to church—and keep going! Sometimes it takes time to feel comfortable and get to know people—that's why we have to keep going. But it's worth it!

Remember, God asks us to do things because they work and they're good for us. Getting involved and helping out, being a part of a church, is good for us. And it feels good knowing we're doing good and helping others. We end up receiving as much as we give. Or more!

So get involved. Go to grow! There's nothing like it.

32